MY DOOMSDAY SAMPLER

MY DOOMSDAY SAMPLER

Poems

SUE OWEN

Louisiana State University Press
Baton Rouge
1999

*My thanks to my family, my friends, and
especially to Thomas Owen for his support
and helpful criticism.*

Copyright © 1999 by Louisiana State University Press
All rights reserved
Manufactured in the United States of America
First printing
08 07 06 05 04 03 02 01 00 99
5 4 3 2 1

Designer: Melanie O'Quinn Samaha
Typeface: Trump Mediaeval
Printer and binder: Edwards Brothers, Inc.

Grateful acknowledgment is made to the editors of the periodicals in which poems in this book originally appeared: *The Denver Quarterly* for "I Think about Ink"; *Harvard Magazine* for "This Candle Lives"; *The Iowa Review* for "Three Peas in a Pod"; *The Journal* for "The Cutting Board" and "The Sorrow and Woe Poem"; *Louisiana Literature* for "The Flea Bites," "How the Truth Hurts," "K is for Kitchen," and "Name Your Poison"; *The Massachusetts Review* for "The Flaw in the Flue" and "To Hell in a Handbasket"; *The New Delta Review* for "Curiosity Kills the Cat," "The Devil's Cookbook," and "Hen's Teeth"; *The New Orleans Review* for "My Doomsday Sampler"; *The New Virginia Review* for "Falling in Love with Gravity"; *The Oregon Review* for "Burnt to a Crisp"; and *Poetry* for "Fire and Brimstone," "These Fireflies," "Total Darkness," and "Written in Blood."

Library of Congress Cataloging-in-Publication Data

Owen, Sue.
   My doomsday sampler : poems / Sue Owen.
      p.   cm.
   ISBN 0-8071-2402-8 (cloth : alk. paper). —ISBN 0-8071-2403-6 (pbk. : alk. paper)
   I. Title.
PS3565.W564M95   1999
811'.54—dc21   99-14900
                                                              CIP

The paper in this book meets the guidelines for permanence and durability of the Committee on Production Guidelines for Book Longevity of the Council on Library Resources. ∞

CONTENTS

I

II

III

MY DOOMSDAY SAMPLER

Then on that day,
those witnesses, the stars,
will blink out.

I

THE FLY IN THE OINTMENT

Look at that bold fly,
spoiling what it has touched
with the strange dirt
it has collected on its body.

The dirt of decay is there,
and germs ready to start
up the passion of disease.
And stink is there, on

this fly's feet, for it walked
where rot had already
welcomed itself, skins
and pits that rot and bones

and the old odor of blood.
And if that fly isn't
despicable enough, it now
struggles to free itself

from what it is, stumbles
and buzzes, as if to lift
itself out of the ointment,
but it stirs itself into

this hell of its own making.
It further buries itself
in its foulness and its fate.
And it finds nothing it

can reach for to save it,
not the thick and sticky
ointment, not the cold jar,
not the stare of our contempt.

FIRE AND BRIMSTONE

The Devil sets fire
to the earth because it
has been bad and
dirtied itself. He laughs

at the dirty water
that reflects back dirty
sky, and the poor dirty
coughing birds that will fall.

The sky itself chokes on
the smoke puffing up
out of the dangerous
chimneys, each one speaking

of the darkness to come
in the blood of man.
Each one breathing poison
until the sun rises and

sets on so many deaths
that the Devil can no
longer keep track of them
and they themselves become

part of the unnamed dirt.
This dirtiness can never
be washed clean, so it
must burn, the Devil thinks.

Burn up until all thought
stops, and the sky stays
red out of sheer anger,
and no angel dares to land.

THORN ON THE ROSE

It has to be like that,
a thorn there so close
to the unfolding beauty,
so close to the color and

odor that dazzle. It
has to assert itself, that
thorn, show its point
off, so that sharpness

and pain are always nearby,
or beauty's story, or
any story, couldn't be told.
So that thorn is doing

its job by being in the way,
when touch comes by
to admire the rose or cut
it. That thorn is standing

up for what needs to be said,
when it pricks the thumb
or draws blood or an ouch.
Pain and beauty always

go together in life like
that, and this is what the
thorn knows, as it hides
behind the green leaf and

waits for the glory to
come, thorn that grows on
the same stem as the rose
but lives a spiteful life.

CHICKEN LITTLE KNEW

Chicken Little knew
a thing or two.
Chicken Little was right.
The stars frown now,

and the sun is a sourpuss
shedding gloom on the land.
The sky is falling.
Clouds stumble before us

and fall and fail us.
Clouds turn up black
and raise their ugly fists,
and the land is afraid.

The sky is falling.
The rainbow tries to crank
out the old ideas of
joy and hope, but that

pot of gold isn't there,
and the rain bites into
the flights of birds, or
the birds are gone, too.

Henny Penny didn't listen
to the warning at hand.
Henny Penny was foolish
not to care if the universe

would crumble right
before her eyes and ours.
The sky is falling.
Chicken Little was right.

OLD POTATO EYES

All they could see,
as they grew in the dirt,
was the darkness that hid
them from the light.

And they could only guess
what else there was
in the world besides
dirt and roots and stones.

And the heaviness like
a lid that held them down.
Above, there was a weather
up there they would

wake into as if opening
their eyes for the first
time, and they would
look up to behold a sky

and the flight of clouds.
And the strange dance
the birds made from tree
to tree to earth. Soon

they would wake into
the light of that world
and see they had too
many eyes to behold all

there was to see and to
learn, and that wisdom again
would seem like the old
sad heaviness settling in.

THAT ONE SQUEAKY WHEEL

You know the saying
that the squeaky wheel
gets all the grease.
The wheel that as it turns

complains, cries out when
it hits a bump in the road,
is the one our attention
turns to, its spokes,

its rim and its hub.
And that one squeaky wheel
complains to us about
too much weight on it,

or the speed, or the rain
that will make it rust,
and it makes us hear
its fragile yet persistent

voice there, spattered by
mud as it squeaks for us.
And isn't all complaining
like that, when we are

grumpy, or sour, or just
plain in one of those foul
moods, and care comes to
comfort us? Isn't care like

a grease to smooth the mind,
so we can roll again like
the other wheels in the company
of silence and happiness?

THE CUTTING BOARD

How the cutting board
is scarred now
with what the knife wrote
as it cut beef, onions,

and loaves of bread.
Every cut is marked
there like a word.
The words "blood" and "pain"

are there, and "death"
and "change" are carved in.
This is the story the knife
wrote if we will read it.

These are the knife's
initials so we can tell who
that great author is.
Think of the inspiration

the knife must have felt
as it was cutting
that chicken in two, or
just cutting off its wings.

Inspiration in itself
is a story, and hard work
is another story, how
the knife daily grew

duller, but let itself be
sharpened so it could go on.
So it could slice better
than before and cut deeper.

DEAD RECKONING

DEAD CENTER I am aiming my
words right at you.
DEAD DOORNAIL I can hammer

you into this door.
DEAD WRONG I will win
this argument we are having.

DEAD CERTAIN I want you
and truth to be on my side.
DEAD WEIGHT Carry your heaviness

to gravity, I don't want it.
DEAD STAR I can only see
your death that is shining.

DEAD NERVES You have been
dead so long, touch can't help.
DEAD SERIOUS I'd rather be

a fool than let you hang around.
DEADWOOD If I had an axe,
I'd stop you and the rot.

DEAD END It is a good thing
you stopped yourself
before it was too late.

DEAD LETTER You end up where
not even the stamps
wanted to send you.

DEADPAN I could take your
expression and make it boil.
DEADLINE I will get to

the end of my rope before you.
DEAD RECKONING This dead sea
will take me there in my boat.

II

PERIOD

I said to the period,
is all of this as final
as it seems?
You are as small as a dying

star, as small as a nail
that has been nailed in
for good. Your eye never
blinks. Your stare,

your world view look set.
Tell me if you have made
up your mind and
don't plan on changing it.

But the period never spoke.
It seemed to be rooted
in the silence where
it had taken seed.

It was the dark moon that
no light in my voice
could ever make shine.
And it preferred what it had

become at the end of
words, where meaning was
told to go back or to
jump off and face certain death.

I knew I was wasting my
breath talking, and that,
from that point on, the period
would never be listening.

THE WORM IN THE APPLE

It thinks as you would
in its world of pulp,
eating and dreaming there,
that life dark but surrounded

by all the spectacle of light.
It bites as you would
a path for itself through
the numbness of days and

never thinks of the harm
it does to that earth of apple,
how rot will set in
like a slow death to follow

it and that the heavy tree
the two of them belong
to is weighted by the worm's
travels and ambition,

and is that much sadder.
It crawls as you would,
taking what belongs to it,
that worm and you digging

deeper into unconcern
as if it were the only cosmos,
greed lighting all the stars,
and time having no way

to stop your own sure pace.
Isn't selfishness like that,
feeding on itself until
all the thoughts grow fatter?

GATHERING NO MOSS

The rolling stone gathers
no moss as it rolls.
This we know, it rolls
like the earth that throws

off the infinite darkness,
rolls through space, so
that time and the glittering
stars cannot catch it.

This we know, it rolls
like blood along the path
to the heart, so that
stillness never dares to

stop it, and so that quick
breath rolls along with it,
the two of them blowing
off the weight of death.

And our rolling stone
rolls because that is all
it knows how to do, and
never thinks about darkness,

stillness, or the growing
intention in the small seed.
of moss, and the plan for
slowness brooding there.

This stone does not think
about foes or woes, any more
than we should; it goes on.
It just keeps on rolling.

THE ANT AND THE GRASSHOPPER

Think of that poor ant,
how it takes those small
steps to accomplish its
smaller makings and follows

the path of its fear to
build a life where it stores
food for the blind winter
already staring at it.

And think how that ant
makes small plans, so
that every detail is filled
up with that scrutiny,

the small minutes that
scurry as that ant keeps
busy, with both its heart
and mind, just to follow

the orders that instinct gives.
And think how there is
nothing else that small
ant can do but obey its

only desire for survival,
and how if you were a carefree
grasshopper you, too, would
laugh at that submission to

work. You, too, would want
to think big and hop joyfully,
and spend your summer singing
of idleness in the grass.

HEN'S TEETH

How rare it would be
to see hen's teeth.
How rare it would be
to see the unseen,

to think the unthought thought.
Then the mind reaches back
for the starlight
that is barely there,

that is so far off one
hopes it into being.
For instance, hen's teeth,
being so rare, they

are unheard of like unseen
planets or moons.
How rare it would be
to see into the possible

the impossible, as if
it had been waiting there
all along, hen's teeth
to punctuate the impossible

with the here and now.
And in the hen house
of possibilities, this hen
and her hen's teeth would

sink into our thoughts.
Example setting example.
Toothmarks to make our words.
Toothmarks of the impossible.

WORK MYSELF TO DEATH

I take my work seriously.
I will work myself
to death,
as the saying goes.

I will work my fingers
down to the bone, until
my bones ache, and
my blood and thoughts run dry.

I will fill page after
page, so that no blank
page stares back
like a rude moon.

I will work because work
is the habit
that I will never break.
And late into the hour,

I will work to get the words out.
Sometimes the work is hard,
hard luck, hard life.
Sometimes the work is easy.

And there is little pay
and plenty of rejection.
And the point on my pencil
grows duller and duller,

like an arrow that makes
an animal bleed
but cannot kill it unless
I sharpen it. I sharpen it.

THE KEY IN THE LOCK

How many times must
the key turn to unlock it,
the lock that holds itself
shut to make the world tight

and to bury the secrets
hidden from the inquiry of day?
How many times must
the key say the words that

make the lock want to
open, so that darkness is
released again like a gift,
and the lock on the door, box,

or house admits another?
Is it too much to expect
this lock to uncurl itself,
to twist and turn and click,

until it no longer grips
what it was asked to protect?
Can this lock, inscrutable
and divine, know the wisdom

of its power, and when to
give it up to the right purpose?
Can the key itself know
all of this and prophesy

the future with its dour stars
and its stumbling shadows,
and convince the lock that
the time for certainty is now?

NAME YOUR POISON

Name them now.
All the poisons that send
fear creeping up your spine.

That make you jump.
That give you the goose bumps.
Poisons so pure

that just the thought of
them could kill.
Snake rattle in your mind,

so to speak.
Spider winding its
web into your thoughts.

Mushroom quick to poison you
with its touch.
How much more can you name

or avoid?
Poisons somewhere now
that are packing their punch,

that are sizing you up.
Whose only goal is to be deadly.
It's more than threat,

more than the thought of
the wolf's tooth at your throat,
and the pile of bones

scattered afterwards. It is
the unknown lurking here.
A choice you make now

that even the stars, that are
dead and that no longer
blink, are watching.

ONE FOOT IN THE GRAVE

But the other foot
is probably more interesting,
right now, where it rests
there in the graveyard,

near its nearly buried friend.
The other foot still
has a chance above the earth
to remember shoes and roads,

and why walking made
it happy, and that there
are destinations filled
with light that it can

still point to, those toes
doing this as they think.
And the other foot feels
that freedom now, even

though its friend has fallen
into the deepest shadows,
where the dirt whispers
its coldness to it and

where the end is almost in
sight, that greatest darkness
eager to claim the two
of them, but not yet.

The other foot claims life.
The other foot will stomp
on death if it dares
to come near and snatch it.

STINKS TO HIGH HEAVEN

It stinks as most things
do because rot sets its
eye upon it, stinks
like fish more than three

days old, stinks like
bad eggs, like bad wine
also gone to hell.
It is the same stink

that lingers near pools
and sewers, then heads
underground, where all rot
seeks darkness, then slinks

out of sight. But when it
stinks here, it rises like
a twisted flame that can do
no good, so it doesn't.

It makes trouble for
noses everywhere, the same
way that evil steps into
our lives when we least

expect it, the way that
all evil is a rot and tries
to undo us, invading what
is pure, stinking up what

is true, making everything
foul, our lives helpless,
so that even the heavens get
a whiff of our awful stink.

III

A POEM CALLED NO

This is about the NO
that is a rock in your road.
You can stop, stumble,
or fall over it.

The NO that is the knot
in your rope and in which
"yes" is hanging
unless you cut it down.

Or the NO that is the fish
that your every question
keeps catching.
You keep throwing that NO

back in the sea
and wait for "yes" to turn up.
But "yes" hasn't shown you
its colors yet.

So NO keeps you company.
You play cards for NO
money and NO one really wins.
This NO that is a relative

to NOthing and NOwhere
helps pass your time.
And you get along fine.
There is NO point to your story.

NO direction it is heading in.
NO reason to complain
about the past or future.
NO reason to complain.

PINCUSHION

You think that it
can take this pain,
all these pins and needles
stuck into it, as still

it does not bleed or cry.
It does not complain about
the sharpness of these
arrows or about the wounds

that never heal because
it tries not to feel them.
It does not complain about
the weight of this

grief, or why you should
want to do this to it,
as you sew, though it
has never done you wrong.

So it carries your pins
and needles into the cloth
of its brain, into the round
head of its thinking,

where pain is the target,
where anguish gathers
the darkness of suffering,
as if it belonged there.

You think that the pincushion
can take this pain, that you
can poke it again and
again, but it can die.

PAVING THE WAY TO HELL

This road is not paved
with stones, the way the
others are, little stones
that clatter under the wheel

grinding them down further,
nor is it paved with plain
dirt that lies flat and
smooth if that same wheel

presses it, nor that dirt
that puffs up a breath of
dust, if it is kicked hard.
This road is special, you

see, because you pave it
with your own good intentions,
and the weather, neither
rain nor cold, nor the heat

from where this road is
headed, ever comes into play.
Only your good intentions
matter here, as if they have

a weight and know the direction.
It is your intentions that
lead you now and all
that you create, which you

think will take you to good,
but, let me tell you,
your special road has already
taken you to that bad turn.

THE SORROW AND WOE POEM

WOE and SORROW, two
that are inseparable.
They both share the O

of OUCH and OW,
though SORROW has two
O's, like eyes that weep.

And they both share
the W of WEARY and
the WEIGHT of the WORLD.

They both share the W
of WISDOM and WORRY.
What they share is

the burden of all our
SORROW and WOE
that they must carry.

But WOE stands alone
with its E, and because
it is a shorter word,

it carries the weight
of EVERYTHING else that
is EAGER to punish it

with pain, and WOE cries
out while SORROW
is moaning and wringing

the two R's of its RAW hands.
I ask you now, could
SORROW be in more pain,

because it is a longer
word, begins with the true
S of all our SADNESS?

THIS MOTH POEM

Even as it flies out
of the dark cloth of night,
this moth wants to be
whole again, wants to

flutter where the light
calls it to meet the flame.
So this moth pulls itself
out of the shadows, out

of the corners of web,
out of that darkness it is
made of, to find the one
star that wants it, too,

to hover near it so that
darkness and light can meet.
And who would warn
this moth not to fly in

so close to the flame?
Who would say "Stay back,"
because the candle
this gives off light must

burn everything it touches,
even this flutter of darkness
that leans towards it
like the quickest flower?

No one answers, as this moth
flies closer to what it
wants, but the flame, as if
to answer, burns brighter.

I THINK ABOUT INK

I think about the dark
blood that ink is,
spilling itself onto the paper,
the blots and puddles

that are words now,
the river of thought that
is going somewhere out
to see what is there.

Ink, like water that lets
itself be rain, or snow,
has its own seasons,
names its path where it goes,

turns corners, jumps,
stands still, but still is words,
as all blood is the dark
word called "life."

I see my life in the ink
and what I think about it.
I think ink is the shadow
of what I am that

keeps following me as if
each word is a foot-
step taken behind my back.
And calls me back to

think about it. Then
I think I know where I am
going when ink flows
along with me through my heart.

THE SKELETONS LAUGH

Once they had breath to
help them carry the weight,
but now they are lighter.
And it's better, too, because

death has locked them into
that perfect grin and they
smile at everything in sight,
everything they haven't

already scared away
with the clacking that their
bones make when they try to
walk out of the graveyard.

But there are other problems,
too, such as how no one
wants them around and they
must hang back in death

and shine there as lonely
as dim moons and far away.
But it could be worse,
they think, at least they

can laugh and be merry
that they have each other
and a place called home,
though it has shrunk and

is quite small. At least
they can tell jokes to
each other, with no fear that
the laughter would kill them.

TOTAL DARKNESS

The light dwindles down
to nothing as
the candle sputters out.
And the darkness begins

to shine its own fury.
Darkness as deep as
the earth is that lays
itself upon the dead

so that they sleep well
and all is quiet for them.
Darkness as deep as
the sky is that takes our

prayers out where
nothing has ever been
found that answers back.
That darkness is what will

happen when the light
of the stars dwindles
out before dawn and all
starlight at last blinks out.

And that light in your
eyes when it dwindles
away, at the end of time,
will join all those

same darknesses that
belong together, that
total darkness of the earth,
the sky, and the soul.

THE SPIDER TO THE FLY

Come into my parlor,
said the spider to the fly.
Come into my web made
out of shadows and dust,

where the lines of fate
intersect to catch you in
their only woven darkness.
Come into my night of

corners and stars and dream,
where you will never wake.
Come into the death that
I spin just for your taking,

certain and bloodless,
the crooked twist of pain,
when you cannot breathe
or fly because you are mine.

And in my parlor, hung
with the mirror of your tears,
I will wait for you and
the collapse of your life

into all the polite niceties
of a slow and morbid struggle,
though we may choose to call
that our gay conversation.

And then, fly, I will taste
you as if you were another
dumb crumb that I consume
with the last sip of my tea.

THIS CANDLE LIVES

This candle lives but once.
And knowing this,
it sheds the tears
of its wax as it burns

down to the black wick.
But as it burns it shines.
It sends the light
flickering out into every

corner of the room where
the dust has gathered
and promised to be dark,
where darkness needs

to be parted and converted
for awhile to goodness.
This candle sends its light
all over the room until

the room glows with that
good knowledge of fire.
And light shines on the
table and the book and on

the face reading these
only words that describe it.
And as the candle lives
by fire and gives

up its body to the burning,
so the light of its soul
will be remembered by
every darkness it touched.

IV

CURIOSITY KILLS THE CAT

The mind steps out
now on little cat's feet
because it can see
better in this dark, this

ganging up of ignorance
that passes for the night,
and inquires around a
corner to see what is

breathing there, what thinks,
or is food for thought.
It might be a gray mouse
or that hint of shadow

that pulls the mind on,
to the end of a branch,
but is nothing but
the flight of a light bird.

And there in that air,
the cat and the mind could
fall down to the danger
of earth and feel it

smack the head like
the most powerful idea
of them all, the one
that curiosity keeps looking

for, and why the mind
takes so many chances.
All along curiosity keeps
pawing around to find death.

CRICKETS

Some summer nights you
can hear them getting all
worked up over this idea
of cheerfulness and song.

Deep in the grasses where
they hide, there is a need
to be heard in the darkness,
even if their voices are

so small they sound
like a door creaking on
its hinge, or the squeak
a drawer makes when

it opens up at last.
It seems as if the damp
air and dew are trying
to hold their song down

out of sheer gravity,
but neither dampness nor
darkness makes them stop.
In fact, the crickets like

to show off their song,
to let it lift up off
the earth the way that
all notes rise to the stars,

and float up through the
thick night, as if their
joy itself were the only
light we needed to follow.

TO BITE THE HAND

Think of those teeth
that bite the hand
that feeds them, those
ungrateful white teeth that

are sharpened, yet miss
the crucial point.
They could be stars that
are so blind they cannot

see the earth beneath.
They could be bright knives
whose only feast seems
to be the blood running.

And why should we
expect these teeth, whose
only thoughts puncture
life, to know better, to

know that the hand, as
gentle as a cloud, comes
to them in peace and caring?
That hand, with its meek

fingers, dares to be near
their bite and danger, and
in its wisdom chances it.
So why can't the sharp teeth

learn, too, that the power
to hurt doesn't have to
happen, not to bite down
so that a scream answers?

PRETTY AT DUSK

You've got to hand it
to that pink doing all it
can to pretty up the scene
right before the dead of

the night sets in, and before
that chill nips at the nose
and fingers to make them
remember all that is in store.

There is that pink spilling
and stretching itself all
over the place until the
low sky is lit with it like

a promise or a smile,
or something so pretty
the stars are going to be
careful before they step out.

They'll want to look their
best, like clean teeth.
But I digress again, and to
get back to that pink, I

think of such a softness,
like the inner glow of a rose
whose heart is happy.
But then I remember that

the situation is sad or worse.
The earth is losing its light
and sinking into a night
from which it cannot recover.

THE FLAW IN THE FLUE

All that stuff about
the flea and the fly
being caught in there is true.
That they were uncertain

about what to do is true, too.
It was a chimney flue
and beneath it there was
an unlit fire waiting while

they thought and decided.
That matter about whether
to flee or to fly also
is relevant to this story,

as escape is also relevant
in times of panic like that,
but in the end they flew.
So this isn't a story

just about cute language,
not just about the small flea
and the fly in the flue,
but about the flaws

that dreams are made of,
imperfections through which
possibilities open and
the world of blue sky appears.

This is about how smart
those two were to use flaws
to undo the death that the
cruel flue wanted for them.

WRITTEN IN BLOOD

What was blood
but a dream circulating,
so that the stars
would swing, and the

wind of the breath would
move, and the mind
would wake to a temporary
knowing that seemed endless?

Why was blood
spinning on course, if
not to make the body
and time seem endless,

to make gravity what
the heart was called to,
the in and out of the voice
itself, that calling

back to the world and
blood running to greet it?
Where was blood going
when it described those

orbits that a life is,
that perfect cycle that
a circle is, as pure as
the moon and as filled with

a light, the red glow
that the blood shines inside
us, so that every word
rising up is filled with it?

K IS FOR KITCHEN

It doesn't matter
if it's been said before.
The knives in this drawer
still dream of a slice of

beef and the blood that
runs away from pain.
And next to them, the spoons
still dream of soups they

could dive into to reach
that chunk of chicken.
Instead, they might come up
with just a noodle.

That's how life goes on.
But the forks, too, want
something solid to poke
until it says, "ouch." Maybe

a piece of pork with
a little crust of fat that
smiles like a slim moon.
And whose job would it

be to attack these meats
if the knife, spoon, and
fork didn't work things out?
How would we eat without

that cut that undoes a life?
That poke that lets the
breath out, that scoop that
says, "Now I will make you mine."

HOW THE TRUTH HURTS

Hurts like a hammer,
and you are the nail,
a dull nail that has to be
hit harder. Hurts

like a knife that twists
once it is in, that
twists just to make sure
you bleed. No, twists

just for the fun of it,
as if pain were another
kind of laughter. And
the truth is just

a joke, this joke.
Hurts like a rope around
the neck, and you do
the hanging, and your

neck snaps like a match.
And the pain is the fire.
That is how the truth hurts.
Hurts like bones broken,

like skin cut, like fever,
the emotions fear and
hate playing tag, anger
playing hide and seek.

The truth is just a game,
but the truth plays
rough. Otherwise, what you
didn't know wouldn't hurt.

THESE FIREFLIES

Now we see them, then
now we don't, these
tiny stars whose only hope
is that they will outlast

the night, if they stick
to it and burn, if they
blink again in the face
of the blind darkness.

And whose will will
win after all as these
fireflies dot and scamp
and burn there, trying

to show us that light
and smallness matter,
even if their own glowing
will soon fade out of sight?

Even if dimness plans
to step in and put out
their gay flit of fire?
We who watch them know

that it is their burning
that always wins, as brief
as it is, as fragile, and
that this kind of magic

stuns even the old crawling
night that dozes, as the
fireflies dance above it,
as if to light up its dream.

KILLING THOSE TWO BIRDS

To kill those two birds
with the same stone requires
quick thinking and a skill.
It requires that those two

birds, where they are flying
in a sky of blank air,
and minding their own business,
must fall together, or where

they are hopping in and out
of a tight bush must drop
dead at the same instant.
Surely, the stone thinks,

this is a difficult and tricky
task that all its weight
and speed, so the saying
goes, must try to accomplish.

This is a deed showing
the importance of efficiency,
good planning and the
strength of the almighty will,

and it is the stone's job
to prove there is nothing,
not even the lives of two
birds, that it cannot stop.

But the stone is thick with
the earth and brooding,
knows nothing of intelligence,
waits for the right hand.

A POEM WITH STARS

In the beginning I wanted
to leave out the stars.
But who could doubt
their sincerity, their

laughter and grimness?
Who could doubt that
they were watching and
even listening, all

eyes and ears, so to speak?
And that every wish
of ours was decided by
them, actually turned

over in the light of their
centuries, and it is for
us at least to mention them?
So I mention now their

sparks that light
the vastness of our nights,
their presence that inhabits
all the loneliness of time.

Our days on earth are
made better because, like
the birds, they are simply
there, shining through

all the doubts and fear
that we can think up.
In any kind of darkness
that we make up, they shine.

V

THE BLACK PEPPER

Even as it sits in
the shaker thinking up
what's wrong with
the world, it is black.

And when it falls asleep
there and dreams, it
is the same thing, the
nightmares are black,

the sky is falling, or
evil is brooding again
in the human heart,
and the vision is black

through and through.
Then the waking pepper
thinks of its grains,
the size of dust and

how they add up to
fill the shaker, and soon
they will be shaken out
to pepper the world with

more black than the
world needs, more doom
sprinkled on all that
will be eaten and lived on.

Pain will thrive and
war and woe and death.
That thought is more than
the black pepper can bear.

SPADEWORK

Things couldn't be more
dismal right now.
The stars are rotting like
fruit not picked in time,

the same way that age
will rot all of us,
which isn't to say that
lying won't help us out.

We could say that the stars
are still right and dazzle,
and wishes come through.
It's true in the darkness

the old lies do
still excite us like hope.
But it's wrong to lie,
and, the way I see it, it

makes things worse.
It makes the truth murky,
and makes it harder to
get around without

bumping into the unknown.
I'd rather not be blind to
what I don't want to see.
I'd rather see life for

what it is, this shortness
of breath between birth
and the coming grave,
and call a spade a spade.

MY DOOMSDAY SAMPLER

A   There is no way to argue
with you. I have seen
your pride. I will stitch
you into this cloth so
that you point to the mirror.

B   I will stitch you round
with greed and your two bellies.

C   I will call you the mouth
that calls for trouble.

D   I will dare to divide you
with the moon
and still see your dark light.

E   You say you were blown east
by the ill wind, but I
will stitch in your lust.

F   I can find no better way
to stitch you than to
follow your arms
that point right to all fear.

G   You are the gulp after
the swallow of gluttony.
So I will stitch you as you are.

H   I have seen your desire
to be a fence, to be two
poles that hold a clothesline,
but no, I will not reward
your envy. I will stitch
you only as an H.

I   You think you are what I am,
but you are wrongheaded.
I will stitch you
without a head.

J   I have seen you jump for joy,
but I do not believe
you are joyous. I will
stitch a lid on your jump.

K   I want to be kind to you
though you kill. I want
to stitch you into this cloth
so that you will keep
your two hands off my neck.

L   You live the life of low
thoughts and are lower than
a snake and a brother to evil.
I will stitch you with
my dark thread as a snake.

M   Maybe you are as magnificent
as a mountain, but I don't
believe it, or make
me believe it.

N   No one understands your slide
from nothing, or why you lean.
I will stitch in
your look of sloth.

O   You open your mouth to say
nothing like a fool.

P   Please let me off your hook.
Let's just say I stitched you
with a big lip and pouting.

Q   You break the circle
the same way you break in here
like a thief. I will stitch
you hanged with your tongue out.

R   Reason is with you, but
you rule it out. You are
rude and stubborn. I will
stitch you to stay
where you planted your feet.

S   I see the silly river you
are that has changed its mind.
My stitch will sink your fish.

T   You stand for trouble.
I cannot get by you without
pricking myself
with this needle. I will
stitch my pain into your T.

U   Watch out. You have left
your begging hand open.
The slap of anger is not money.
I stitch you and the
V   as vulnerable.

W   Watch out. There are deadly
sins everywhere and cut-
throats, liars, and cheats.
Don't change. I don't want
to stitch you in wrong.

X   You are the crossroads
here between good and evil.
I will stitch you in
as the X that marks the spot.

Y   I have seen your remorse.
I will stitch you as
the two hands before prayer.

Z   You end what was begun
with a sleep or
the sneeze of a doomsday.
I will stitch you last
with the dark star of a knot.

FALLING IN LOVE WITH GRAVITY

It is the same for them,
the grave diggers, as
their shovels slap and kiss
the earth to bury their

treasure in the deep.
They have fallen in love
with gravity, as the dead
fall out of step with

time, fall out of tune,
fall out of luck in the end.
And isn't it the same
for us, who rise out of

our births to climb
that ladder of days up
and away from darkness,
that the knowledge of that

old love of gravity pulls
us back and slowly down?
Doesn't the weight of
our bones know it, as they

bravely carry us on,
that there was another love
earlier that the heart
pushes against, but can't forget?

Isn't gravity like that,
calling us to complete ourselves,
calling us back to that
wholeness from which we came?

THE BIG QUESTION MARK

They say that the meaning
of life is a big question
mark, an unanswered
question mark that rises

above the flame of our lives
like scattered smoke.
A question mark that rises
to leave us for the stars,

then circles back to see
us on earth still here,
the dot of our voice still
asking the questions beneath

its curved ear. Is the
question mark listening to
what we ask it, the why,
the how, the where and when?

Does the question mark care
if we want it to catch an
answer with that big
hook that could be a hand?

Does the question mark,
that looks like a head on
a stem, think about us, or
understand what it means

to never receive an answer?
No, the question mark only
does what it is so good at.
Just hangs in the silent air.

THREE PEAS IN A POD

All they can think now
is how snug they are,
lined up in there, one,
two, three, the walls

green, and how their heads
put together are better
than one, and when
they doze, the pod is like

a ship crossing a smooth
green sea that is eternity.
But put back in time,
they wake again to their

smallness, their swaying
on the stem, and their
ripening that will take
them to the kitchen where

all pea shucking begins.
As their heads pop into
that pan, they will bounce
out of their snugness

into the pain of a metal
bottom, the pain of water
that will float them to
a boil, the pain of fire.

And that old snugness,
as frail as a dream,
will think of them when
they scream above the flame.

THE FLEA BITES

It hops in the thickness
of fur until it lands
in the cat's ear and bites.
And there it annoys as

if it were paid to do this,
and there it lounges around
thinking up more ways
to make trouble, as if this

biting while the cat tries
to scratch it were not enough.
Then there is the cat's tail
left to bite, the belly,

and, thinks the flea, that
difficult place behind the neck.
But for now the flea sits
tight, so to speak, in the ear

practicing its hopping,
and whispering to the cat
all of its irritating plans.
This is the flea's privilege,

isn't it, to do as it pleases,
even if it doesn't please
the cat, and to act out
the little harm given to it?

This is the flea's place
in the order of evil, isn't
it, and the way that all
of us must endure that pain?

BURNT TO A CRISP

You say you are ash
now, just a flutter
of grayness that breath
or the wind catches,

and that now all you
can do is fly or crumble.
You say that fire did
this to you, consumed

you beyond belief, and
that flame was never
your friend, though
more light is what you

always thought you wanted
and you called to fire
to come and made
it your only desire.

But now there is this
coldness you live with,
and your own words
that rise faint and white.

Now there is this whisper
as you speak to us from
the grate and the charred
log that did not catch.

Your voice to us is
only a stale smoke now.
You are nothing and your
nothingness will not pass.

TO HELL IN A HANDBASKET

As long as you are going
to hell, you may as
well go in a handbasket,
packed in like an ugly

loaf of bread, or like
a few homely potatoes
tucked by its side, or onions
that, as they go, stink

to high heaven and rattle
their dry skins like a cry.
And the ride is quick
over the bumpy road to hell

from the market in that
handbasket, and you are stuffed
into it and could not
escape your fate, the same

way that the basket is
woven into its final shape
and cannot escape its calling.
And there is a talking flame

that you in the handbasket
can already hear, though
you cannot see it yet.
And there is a heat in hell

this flame is talking about
that wants to feed on you,
when you arrive at that
devouring fire of its kitchen.

THE FLY ON THE WALL

To be that small,
and still to hear and see
everything that goes on in
that room where others try

to keep their secrets hidden.
To hold that place on
that wall as your own,
your feet stuck there by

a stickiness of your making,
and your wings folded in
so tight the others think
you are just another spot.

But you are as tall as
their wall now from where
you observe the habits of
space, the gatherings of a

chair, a rug, and a table,
and the voices that time
unlocks with each tick.
And your fly's eyes,

like round worlds themselves,
take in the whispering
details and shadow truths,
that spell and spill and tell.

Isn't that the fly's calling,
to know its place in smallness?
To be that unimportant, even
to crawl, but to know all?

THE DEVIL'S COOKBOOK

This book must be eternal.
It's covered
with the fingerprints
of messy cooks, but
we can read
past the spills and smears.
We can put on our aprons
and follow the Devil
down the page.
He will introduce us
to the A to Z of delectables,
the bats and demons
as appetizers, hot
brimstone soups, and flaming
desserts that rise heavenward.
Turn to main courses,
and we'll see that pain
can be measured out
so that cups and spoons
make any dish turn out right.
And however it must be
cooked, there is plenty of heat.
Sometimes here
the meats, especially,
don't cook, but burn.
And that, the Devil instructs
us, is the main drawback
to this art,
not to singe, not to turn
anything to ash very quickly,
but to roast, broil, or
boil, in spite of protest.
And to use generously
the sharp vocabulary of spices.